THE AGE OF BLISS–5

ALI
IBN ABI TALIB

ZEKERIYA ULAŞLI

NEW JERSEY • LONDON • FRANKFURT • CAIRO

TUGHRA
BOOKS

Copyright © 2015 by Tughra Books

18 17 16 15   1 2 3 4

Translated by Asiye Gülen
Edited by Clare Duman

Published by Tughra Books
345 Clifton Ave., Clifton,
NJ, 07011, USA
www.tughrabooks.com

Library of Congress Cataloging-in-Publication Data

Ulasli, Zekeriya.
[Hazreti Ali. English]
Ali ibn Abi Talib / Zekeriya Ulasli ; translated by Asiye Gülen ; edited by Clare Duman.
pages cm. -- (The age of bliss ; 5)
ISBN 978-1-59784-374-4 (alk. paper)
1. 'Ali ibn Abi Talib, Caliph, approximately 600-661--Juvenile literature. 2. Caliphs--Biography--Juvenile literature. I. Gülen, Asiye. II. Duman, Clare. III. Title.
DS38.4.A5U4313 2015
953'.02092--dc23
[B] 2015013469

ISBN: 978-1-59784-374-4

Printed by
Imak Ofset, Istanbul - Turkey

TABLE OF CONTENTS

Under the Protection
of the Noble Prophet

It was summer in Mecca and people were suffering, not only from the searing heat but also from poverty. All the people were experiencing hardship, including Abu Talib. Every day he walked through the bazaar looking for trade opportunities, but nothing came up. The burden of providing for his family and six children was increasing each day.

Seeing the difficult situation that Abu Talib was in, our dear Prophet, peace and blessings be upon him, looked for ways in which he could help him. He visited his uncle, al-Abbas, may Allah be pleased with him, and suggested, "O uncle, you know your brother and my uncle, Abu Talib, is in difficulty. How can we help him?"

"Your thoughts are very good," al-Abbas responded. "Do you have any ideas?"

"Yes," replied Prophet Muhammad, peace and blessings be upon him, "but ... I don't know how it could happen."

"Tell me! Whatever you are thinking, I'm sure it is a good idea."

"I mean the children," continued Prophet Muhammad, peace and blessings be upon him, "What if you take care of one of them, and I take care of another?"

"That's a very good idea," said al-Abbas. "Let's go now to Abu Talib and suggest it."

The noble Prophet and al-Abbas went together to Abu Talib's house. On arrival they knocked and entered and the beloved Prophet explained why they had come. Al-Abbas tried to convince him. Hearing their suggestion, Abu Talib became very emotional. When the blessed Prophet was just a child, he had taken him into his home and offered him his protection. Now the Messenger of Allah was offering the same for his child. He didn't know how to respond. Finally agreeing, he said, "It will be how you say but, I want to keep Akil with me."

The noble Prophet took five-year old Ali, may Allah be pleased with him, and Abbas took Jafar, may Allah be pleased with him. Together the four of them happily left Abu Talib. And so it was that from a very young age, Ali was raised in the noble Prophet's house in the best way possible.

That period in Mecca was one of the darkest it had seen. The traders in the bazaar were renowned for lying and most people tried to steal the belongings of others. The rich people didn't help the poor but, instead, enjoyed humiliating them. This behavior greatly disturbed the noble Prophet and he often wondered how he could rectify the situation. At the same time, he protected Ali from what was around him and ensured he grew up with good manners.

I Believe

*I*n the five years since he had moved to live with the Messenger of Allah, Ali had learned to be faithful, to keep his word, to protect the goods that were entrusted to him, to help the poor and to show respect to all people.

He was now ten years old, with black eyes, dark skin and, according to his friends, of average height.

One evening, sitting in his room, it occurred to him that there was something different about the Messenger of Allah, peace and blessings be upon him, but he wanted to find the right time to ask him about it. He hadn't seen him for a few days, but today he was there and Ali saw this as his opportunity to reveal what was on his mind.

Approaching the blessed Prophet's room, he knocked at the door. When there was no answer, he knocked again, but again there was no answer. Full of curiosity, he opened the door and saw the Messenger of Allah and his wife Khadija, may Allah be pleased with her, making strange movements; prostrating on the floor, then standing, then bending. Even more curious, Ali entered the room and sat quietly in a corner, watching their movements. When they finished, he asked them what they were doing.

"We are praying," replied the noble Prophet.

"What is praying?" asked Ali.

"It is worshipping Allah, Who created us and everything, to gain His pleasure," explained the Messenger of Allah.

"Who is it that created us?"

"The one and only Allah. He has no partner, nor is He similar to anyone. He created everything and each one of us. Our food and drink comes from him. He has power over everything."

"You mean, He created us?"

"Yes, you, me, everyone and everything," the noble Prophet answered.

"If I believe in Him, what will happen?" asked Ali.

"Allah will love you and reward you with Paradise. Tell me now, do you believe in the one Allah?"

"Yes, I believe in Him. Because you would never tell a lie. But, if you will permit me, I would like to ask my father's permission first."

Everything that Ali had heard from the Messenger of Allah was new to him. He couldn't accept it all at once. The noble Prophet said to him, "If you believe in what I told you, become Muslim. If not, don't tell anyone what you heard or saw."

"OK, I won't tell anyone," promised Ali.

That night, Ali thought for a long time about what the noble Prophet had explained to him. The next morning, he woke and ran happily to find him. "I believe the things you told me yesterday," he said.

"Did you ask your father for permission?" asked the Messenger of Allah.

Ali answered with the wisdom of an adult, "My dear uncle, did Allah ask my father permission before

He created me? Why should I ask for permission when I want to believe in Him?"

"Then, repeat what I say," said the noble Prophet. "I bear witness that there is no deity but Allah and I bear witness that Muhammad is His servant and Messenger."

Ali repeated the declaration of faith after the beloved Prophet and became the third Muslim after Khadija and Abu Bakr, may Allah be pleased with them.

Go On
Your Way

*A*bu Talib was very fond of his nephew, peace and blessings be upon him. He had heard people saying that he went to the Cave of Hira and stayed there in a cave for months. He had also heard that he was now calling the people around him to believe in the one and only Allah. But, he had not yet heard that his son, Ali, had become a Muslim.

Sometimes, he discussed Muhammad's, peace and blessings be upon him, situation with his wife, Fatima, may Allah be pleased with her. She was concerned about him but was sure that her nephew wouldn't do something wrong. However, she was afraid of what might happen to him.

One day, at lunchtime, Fatima was returning from visiting a neighbor when she saw her son, noble Ali, and our beloved Prophet, peace and blessings be upon him, leaving Mecca. She informed Abu Talib, pleading, "Do whatever you can and find out where they are going."

"Don't worry," replied Abu Talib. "You know very well that our nephew has never done anything wrong."

"I know, but I'm concerned about it. Ali is with him and he is just a child. What if something happens to him?"

The next day, Abu Talib left the city to try and find them. He tracked them as far as the Valley of Dub, then he saw his son and our dear Prophet, peace and blessings be upon him. "What are they doing here?" he asked himself.

From a distance, he stood and watched them. They were making strange movements that he couldn't understand, so he decided to ask his nephew about them. As they finished praying, Abu Talib left his hiding place. Seeing his father approaching, Ali panicked.

"Don't worry, my son, I won't harm you," Abu Talib reassured his son. "I was just curious about what you are doing here."

Standing up, the noble Prophet offered him a place to sit. "Please uncle, I'm listening to you. What would you like to know," he asked him.

"May I ask you why you bent down and then stood upright and made such movements?"

"We were praying to Allah," the noble Prophet answered.

"Are you speaking about the new religion?"

"Yes, uncle! This is the religion of Allah, the angels and the Prophets. It is the religion of our forefather, Abraham. Allah the Almighty has commissioned me to inform others about Him and spread the religion. Come and believe in Allah. Come and become a Muslim," the noble Prophet entreated his uncle.

"What about our ancestors?" answered Abu Talib. "Won't they ask what we've done with the religion they entrusted to us?"

"They were on the wrong path, uncle. Can idols made with our own hands really be the gods for us?

Please, become Muslim and enter the true religion of Allah."

"No, nephew," came Abu Talib's reply. "I can't refuse the religion of my ancestors. But, until I die, I will support and protect you."

Then, turning to his son, Ali, he asked, "Did you also become Muslim like your uncle?"

"Yes, father," Ali answered. "I believe in the one and only Allah, and I believe that my uncle, Muhammad, is His Messenger."

"He will always call you to the true and good path. Continue on your way, my son," Abu Talib told his son.

Turning and leaving, Abu Talib walked directly home. Fatima was waiting for him, full of questions as soon as he entered the house. "What happened? What were they doing there? Is there something to worry about?"

"O wife, stop your questions. Let me come inside first."

"Tell me about my son. Is he alright?" Fatima insisted.

"You won't let me draw a breath! Your son is fine. He is with our nephew. As we discussed, our nephew is calling people to follow the right path and to believe in the one and only Allah. Ali is with him. There is nothing to worry about."

"What do you think about this?" asked Fatima.

"I think he would never do anything wrong," Abu Talib replied.

"So you believe in what our nephew says?"

"I agree with everything he says, but I can't enter his religion. I can't have people telling me that I left the religion of my ancestors."

"I also think the same way," answered Fatima.

The two of them went out into the yard to do their work.

The Idols

The Messenger of Allah often visited the Ka'ba which, at that time, was home to many idols. One day he was visiting the Ka'ba with Ali and, noticing that there was no one around to see them, he said, "What do you say, Ali? Shall we take down these idols that provide no benefit to anyone?"

"Yes, let's take them down, Allah's Messenger," agreed Ali.

Both of them tried to reach the idols, but they were too high up. The noble Prophet said to Ali, "Bend down and let me climb onto you. Perhaps I'll be able to reach them that way."

The beloved Prophet climbed onto Ali's shoulders and tried to remove the idols, but he still couldn't reach them. "I couldn't reach them, Ali," he said. "You climb onto my shoulders instead."

Ali lowered the Messenger of Allah to the ground, then climbed onto his shoulders. At that moment, he felt so high up he imagined he could even reach the stars in the heavens. Ali reached up and took down all the idols, throwing them to the floor where they shattered into pieces. After all the idols had been broken, Ali and the noble Prophet left the Ka'ba.

Hijra
(Migration)

The number of people accepting Islam was increasing every day. This angered the polytheists who began torturing the Muslims and trying to force them to renounce Allah and His Prophet. The torture had reached an unbearable level and the Muslims asked the noble Prophet to permit them to move to a safe place where they could practice their religion without being oppressed.

One day, the Messenger of Allah announced the good news that Allah had given permission for them to make the *Hijra* (migration) to Medina. From that day, leaving all their belongings behind in Mecca, the Muslims began to emigrate to Medina.

This migration disturbed the tranquility of the polytheists who imagined the Muslims would grow in strength in Medina and would take revenge them. Some of the Meccan leaders met to discuss the situation. "Did you hear, the Medinan residents are welcoming the Muslims and looking after them very well?" one of them said.

"Yes, we've heard the same. It seems they will proliferate there," answered another.

Another man chimed in, "It's possible that Muhammad will also emigrate to Medina. This is the biggest risk. If he emigrates and joins the others, we will never prevail against them. We must do everything we can to keep him here."

"What can we do?" asked another man.

Abu Jahl, one of the biggest enemies of the Muslims, stood up. Everyone turned towards him as he said, "It's easy. We'll kill him, and then we'll be rid of him for good."

"Do you really think his relatives would let the murderer live?"

Laughing insidiously, Abu Jahl replied, "No they wouldn't, but I have a plan."

"Tell us," they all replied.

Abu Jahl paused and looked at the people around him. They all waited, anxiously anticipating what this plan could be. Then, Abu Jahl spoke, "We will choose one person from each clan. Each must be able to handle a sword well. They will surround his house and as soon as he leaves, they will set upon him and kill him. No one will know who the killer was and therefore, no one will be able to find the killer."

One of the men in the room shouted out, "This is quite clever!"

Excited, the polytheists applauded Abu Jahl. Then, they started making preparations to carry out the plan, imagining that it was perfect and couldn't fail.

Learning of the plan from the Archangel Gabriel, the noble Prophet started to prepare to migrate to Medina. Before he left, he had many things in his safekeeping that needed to be returned to their owners. Calling Ali to assist him, he told him he had received permission from Allah to migrate and that he would be setting out that night with Abu Bakr, may Allah be pleased with him. He asked Ali to sleep in his bed so as not to attract the attention of

the polytheists and Ali accepted this duty with pleasure. The Messenger of Allah was very pleased and
said to Ali, "Wrap yourself in my green dress so that
no one will harm you."

The sun had set and it was dark outside. The
polytheists surrounded the blessed Prophet's house;
some were under the windows, others were at the
garden gate and the front door. Saying goodbye to
Ali, the noble Prophet prayed to Allah, asking Him
to protect his cousin. Before he left the house, he
read the first verse of Surah Ya-Sin from the Qur'an,
then, taking a handful of earth from the ground, he
blew on it and scattered it in the direction of the
polytheists. No one saw him leave the house.

After waiting for a few hours and not seeing anyone leave the house, the polytheists became impatient.
"I don't think he'll come out," one of them said.

"He'll leave eventually," replied another.

They continued waiting. After a while, a man,
wondering about this strange situation, approached
them and enquired, "Who are you waiting for?"

"For Muhammad," they answered.

"But, he isn't at home," the man said. "I saw him walking in the street."

"Are you joking?" the polytheists cried. "We've been waiting here for hours. It's impossible that he left without any of us seeing him."

The man was adamant, "I told you, I saw him in the street."

"You say you saw him, but is this the truth?" they retorted. "We'll break down the door and look inside. Then, we'll see if you are being honest."

The polytheists broke down the door of the blessed Prophet's house and went inside. Looking at the bed, they could see someone lying on it. "The man lied," they whispered. "Look, he is still in bed."

Unsheathing their swords, they got ready to attack and kill the noble Prophet. One of them pulled back the blanket. Just as they were ready to lunge forward, they jumped back in surprise. It wasn't the blessed Prophet lying in the bed, it was Ali.

"Where is Muhammad?" they shouted angrily.

"I don't know!" replied Ali.

"How can you say you don't know?"

"I really don't know! He will be wherever he wants to be," insisted Ali.

However much they pushed him, Ali wouldn't say a word about the noble Prophet's whereabouts. Furious that their mission had failed, the polytheists left the house.

Waiting for news that their perfect plan had succeeded, the other polytheists were sorely disappointed. They forgot that the real plan-maker is Allah the Almighty.

The following day, Ali returned the goods that had been entrusted to the noble Prophet to their rightful owners. When he had completed this duty, he set out to join the blessed Prophet in Medina.

The Brotherhood

On leaving Mecca, the noble Prophet and Abu Bakr spent three days and nights in Cave Thawr which was near the city. This cave lay in the opposite direction to Medina. When they left the cave, they continued their journey, this time walking towards Medina.

Ali was also making his way towards Medina. After a long journey, he caught up with the Messenger of Allah and Abu Bakr in a village called Quba, close to Medina. Continuing their journey at a rapid pace, Ali began to be disturbed from the sores that covered his feet. After a while, they burst and he could no longer walk. Noticing he wasn't nearby, the noble

Prophet asked the people beside him, "Where is Ali? Call him to come to me."

"He can't walk, O Allah's Messenger," one of them replied.

The Messenger of Allah went to find Ali and, seeing the poor state of his feet, was moved to tears. He rubbed the soles of Ali's feet with his hands and asked Allah to heal them. A little while later, Ali's pain had disappeared.

The Companions stayed in a village to rest for a while, then continued walking towards Medina. Eager to be the first to sight the noble Prophet, all the Medinan residents were waiting excitedly at the gate of the city. Their arrival in Medina was glorious.

To help the emigrants settle in Medina, the beloved Prophet declared the Muslims and the Medinans as brothers. This encouraged a sense of brotherhood in the new community and ensured practical assistance for those who had left everything behind in Mecca.

When it came to finding a brother to pair Ali with, there was no one left. Feeling sad about this situation, Ali discussed it with the noble Prophet.

"Everyone has found a brother except for me," he said. "There is no one left for me to establish brotherhood with."

Smiling, the Messenger of Allah put his hand on Ali's shoulder and asked, "Do you want to be my brother on earth and in Paradise?"

Ali couldn't believe his ears. He was so happy, he could hardly breathe and without hesitating for a second, he answered, "O Messenger of Allah, who could refuse such an offer?"

The Third
Person

One day, the noble Prophet was sitting against a wall when he was joined by his friends, Abu Bakr and Umar, may Allah be pleased with them. After talking for a while, the beloved Prophet suddenly announced, "Both of you have been promised a place in Paradise. Also, whoever comes along now will be the third person who is promised Paradise."

The three friends began to wait to see who the next person would be. Soon, they heard some footsteps approaching and the noble Prophet prayed, "O Allah, if it is Your will, make it Ali who is coming."

Indeed, the person approaching them was Ali and the Messenger of Allah was very happy. He presented him with a two-bladed sword which he named, Dhulfiqar. Ali was overjoyed to receive such a gift from the most worthy human being. "Beloved Allah," he prayed. "Please allow me to use this sword in the way of You and Your religion."

From that day forwards, Ali protected his sword as if it was part of his own body and waited for the opportunity to use it. Finally, the anticipated moment arrived. The polytheists declared war on the Muslims and intended to completely eliminate them.

The battlefield was located at the water wells of Badr. Dressed in armor, the polytheists arrived on horses and camels, outnumbering the Muslims by three to one.

Looking at the enemy, the noble Prophet prayed, "O Allah, if these few believers die, there will be no one left to believe in You until Judgment Day. O my Lord, grant me the glory You have promised me."

The two armies faced in other in silence. After a while, three polytheists moved forward to the center of the battlefield and shouted, "Is there no one to oppose us?"

The Messenger of Allah indicated to three people, including Ali, to step forwards, saying to them, "May Allah be with you."

Ali had been preparing for this moment for a long time. He prayed to Allah saying, "O Allah, please allow me to use this sword in the way of You and Your religion."

Ali approached the battlefield with his two comrades. After a short fight, he defeated the enemy, fulfilling his duty successfully. His comrades, one of whom was Hamza, may Allah be pleased with him, were also victorious.

Thus, the Muslims won the first round. The noble Prophet, wishing to spread the Name of Allah throughout the world, was relieved and happy. This was a war that must be won.

On the other side of the battlefield, the polytheists were despondent after their humiliating defeat in the one-on-one fights. They began to attack with a vengeance. The battle was long and difficult. Ali performed his duty like a hero, fighting bravely with his sword. The enemy lost many warriors, including Abu Jahl. They suffered an unforgettable defeat.

After the battle, the noble Prophet and the Muslims gave thanks to Allah for their victory.

A Young Hero

The polytheists still wished to eliminate the Muslims from Arabia. Assembling an army of three thousand, they marched towards Medina. When they arrived, they came across a wide trench surrounding the city that was completely unexpected. They had never seen such a wide trench and had no idea what to do.

"What will we do now?" asked one of the men.

"We should look for a way to cross it," replied another.

"Assume we find a way over," began another, "what will happen to us when we cross?"

The first man thought a minute, then said, "Of course, we won't all cross at once. First, we will send our best warriors, then the rest of us will cross."

Everyone agreed to this idea and they began searching for a place to cross the trench. After a long search, they found a place that was not as deep as the rest. Some of the bravest from among them passed over first, one of whom was Amr ibn Abdiwud, renowned for being as strong as a hundred men.

As soon as he had passed over the trench, Amr shouted, "Is there no one brave enough to fight me?"

No one replied, but Ali couldn't wait and said, "O Messenger of Allah, I can fight him."

The noble Prophet knew that Amr was almost unbeatable. "This is Amr," he said to Ali. "Stay in your place."

Amr shouted out, even more loudly this time, "Does no one have the courage to fight me? Doesn't anyone want to go to that place Paradise that you talk about?"

Amr intended to infuriate the Muslims into action. Ali, unable to restrain himself, couldn't bear the polytheist's taunts, "O Messenger of Allah," he entreated, "let me fight him."

"Sit down, Ali," the noble Prophet replied again. He seemed to want a more experienced man to confront Amr.

Amr resumed his taunts, continuously mocking them, shouting and reciting poetry because no one had the courage to fight him.

Ali, not able to stand this anymore, once more addressed the beloved Prophet, "Let me fight him, even if he is Amr."

This time, the Messenger of Allah agreed. Dressing Ali himself in a double layer of armor he said, "Go Ali. Allah bless you."

Ali approached his enemy and stood in front of him. Looking at the young man in front of him, Amr asked condescendingly, "Who are you?"

"Ali, son of Abu Talib."

Amr burst into laughter. "Your father is my good friend," he said. "Go back to your place. Is there no one else brave enough to fight me?"

"Of course there are many," Ali answered, "but I want to fight you."

Amr saw that Ali was little more than a child. Dismounting from his horse he attacked him so violently, Ali's sword split in two with one blow from Amr's sword. The tip of Amr's sword, wounded Ali's face. Ali immediately retaliated striking Amr's shoulder with his sword. Amr was fatally wounded. He sank to the ground and as he died Ali and the Muslims shouted, "**Allahu akbar**, Allah is the greatest."

When the polytheists saw that their strongest warrior was defeated and dying on the ground, they was shocked. The Muslims were delighted.

After Amr, more polytheists passed over the trench and many of them fought Ali. None of them could withstand the blows from his sword and they fled. Another of the polytheist's famous warriors, Nawfal, passed over the trench and fought Ali. As he tried to flee, he fell into the trench.

Next, another fearsome warrior stepped forwards but, after a short time, he fell on his knees in front of Ali. Ali raised his sword to strike the final blow and the man spat in his face. Ali immediately lowered his sword and put it in its sheath. Shocked, the man asked him, "Why didn't you kill me?"

Ali replied, "When I fought you, it was for the sake of Allah. As soon as you spat in my face, I became angry and my ego was awakened. If I kill you now it will be because of my ego, not for the sake of Allah. That's why I didn't kill you."

The man couldn't believe what he heard. What kind of religion was this that stopped someone killing when the ego was awakened? He was so impressed he told Ali that he wanted to become Muslim.

On the other side of the trench, the rest of the polytheists didn't know what to do. They had no choice but to wait, but the long wait made them weary and many gave up. The army had almost dispersed.

Winter was approaching. The few remaining polytheists were camped outside Medina. One morning, a fierce desert storm appeared from nowhere destroying their tents and everything around them. The demoralized polytheists gave up their fight and fled.

I Cannot Erase It

The noble Prophet and the Muslims were on their way to Mecca to make a pilgrimage and circumambulate the Ka'ba when the polytheists blocked their way. Telling them that they didn't come to fight, the Messenger of Allah offered to make an agreement with them.

"Let's live in peace with one another," he said. "If you don't accept my offer, I will fight you for the sake of Allah until I die."

The polytheists finally decided to make an agreement. The noble Prophet called Ali to write down the terms, "Write!" he commanded him.

Taking a pencil, Ali began to write, 'In the Name of Allah, the All-Merciful, the All-Compassionate."

The polytheist's representative, Suhayl, at once objected loudly, saying, "What does that mean? 'All-Compassionate and All-Merciful.' If we believed in Allah, we would not be fighting you."

With the intention of making peace, the noble Prophet didn't want anything to prevent the agreement. "Write that the agreement is between Muhammad, the Messenger of Allah and Suhayl, son of Amr," he instructed Ali.

Ali was upset by this but did what the Messenger of Allah told him. As he was writing, he heard Suhayl objecting again, "Don't write 'the Messenger of Allah,'" he said. "If we accepted that he was the Messenger of Allah, we wouldn't fight you! Write that the agreement is between Muhammad, son of Abdullah, and Suhayl, son of Amr."

The noble Prophet agreed, but Ali was not willing to erase what he'd written. He turned to the Messenger of Allah imploring with his eyes, *"How can I do this?"*

The beloved Prophet, however, knew that if he could make this agreement many more people would hear about this beautiful religion. He answered Ali's look saying, "Erase it and write what Suhayl said."

Ali protested, "How can I erase the name I'm trying to spread at every opportunity? I can't do it."

The noble Prophet asked Ali to point out the words, then, without speaking he crossed them out himself. He told Ali to write "son of Abdullah" in their place. Ali reluctantly complied. Ali's actions proved his deep and sincere love for the Messenger of Allah, peace and blessings be upon him, was made very happy by this.

The agreement stated that there would be no more fighting between the Muslims and the Meccan polytheists for a period of ten years. The Muslims would be able to circumambulate the Ka'ba the following year. If a Meccan became Muslim and moved to Medina, he would be sent back.

The Muslims felt that the terms of the agreement were very harsh. The noble Prophet, however, could see the benefit of the agreement for the future of the religion. With an end to the hostilities, Muslims would be free to travel wherever they wanted, people would see the beauty of Islam and the religion would spread. By signing the agreement, the Meccans were recognizing the existence of the Islamic government.

The Muslims were sorely disappointed that they had to leave without visiting the Ka'ba and couldn't see the benefit of the agreement. However, the revelation of Surah al-Fath (the Conquest) giving them the good news of a future victory relieved their minds.

So Much Goodness

One day, the Messenger of Allah and his Companions were sitting and talking together when one of them asked, "O Allah's Messenger, we know you love Ali very much. Can you explain why?"

"You will understand shortly," replied the noble Prophet and sent one of them to fetch Ali.

Meanwhile, the Messenger of Allah asked his Companions a question, "If you doing something good for someone and they do something bad to you, what would you do?"

"We would again do something good for him."

"What if he then did something bad to you again," the noble Prophet asked.

"We would do something good for him again."

"And, what if he did another bad thing to you? What would you do?"

The Companions bent their heads in response to this question, meaning, "*We couldn't continue doing something good for him.*"

Then, Ali arrived and greeted the Messenger of Allah. The noble Prophet asked Ali the same question that he had asked his Companions just a few minutes earlier. "Ali, if you do something good for something and he responds by doing something bad to you, what would you do?"

"I would do something good for him," responded Ali.

"And if he then did something bad to you again?"

"I would do something good for him," said Ali.

"And if he again did something bad to you?"

"I would do something good for him again."

The noble Prophet questioned Ali seven times, each time asking the same question and Ali answered with the same answer each time.

At last the Companions said, "We understand now why you love Ali so much, Allah's Messenger."

The Flag

*I*t was the year 629 C.E. and the sixth year since the migration to Medina. One night, the beloved Prophet, together with an army of one and a half thousand men, set out for Khaybar Castle.

The inhabitants of the castle were the Jews of Khaybar who took every opportunity to provoke the Muslims and spent great efforts to turn the Meccan polytheists and other Arab tribes against them. To put a stop to this ongoing sedition, the Muslims intended to conquer the castle. However, this would not be an easy battle as the castle was situated on top of a high hill making it difficult to approach and attack.

When the Jews woke up in the morning, they were shocked to see the large Muslim army surrounding the castle. They closed the door hurriedly and prepared their defenses. The Muslims held the castle under siege for days, but the Jews refused to surrender.

One day, the Messenger of Allah gathered his Companions and said, "Tomorrow, I'll give one of you the flag and Allah will grant us victory through that person. This man loves Allah and His Messenger and Allah and His Messenger love him."

Could there be a greater honor than this? All the Companions eagerly waited until morning, so excited they couldn't sleep that night. Everyone was wondering if it would be he who would get the flag.

Early the next morning, the moment for the announcement arrived. Full of excitement, the men gathered around the noble Prophet, each hoping to hear his own name. The Messenger of Allah looked from one to the other but didn't say anything. The person he was looking for was not there. Then he asked, "Where is Ali?"

It was apparent that Ali would be the one to carry the flag. "Ali is ill," one of the Companions replied. "He has a problem with his eyes."

Hearing this news, everyone felt renewed hope. Maybe there was still a chance for one of them to carry the flag. However, the noble Prophet said to them, "Bring Ali to me."

Ali was brought before the Messenger of Allah having lain in bed for a few days. The noble Prophet rubbed Ali's eyes with his holy saliva and at once, Ali's eyes were not only healed, he could see even better than before his illness.

The flag was handed to Ali who was the envy of all the Companions. Who wouldn't wish to be in his shoes? Receiving the flag, Ali asked the beloved Prophet, "Shall I fight until they accept Islam?"

The Messenger of Allah replied, "First, you shall invite them to Islam. If they refuse, then you can fight them." He added, "O Ali, know this for sure, if one of them accepts Islam through you, it is more valuable than you donating thousands of camels in the way of Allah."

No other words could have motivated Ali more. Taking the flag and the command of the army, he started the battle. Three Muslims and three Jews stepped forward to fight, the Muslims defeating the Jews one by one. After this, the Jews' most infamous warrior, Marhab, came forward wearing his double-coated armor and shouting angrily, "Is there no one to oppose me?"

Ali unsheathed his sword and confronted him. This was not the first time Ali found himself in this situation. He was the one who had defeated Amr, the Meccan with the strength of one hundred men. Marhab's final destiny was no different to Amr's. After a short time he was laid out on the ground with one strike of Ali's sword.

Seeing this, the Messenger of Allah called to his Companions, "You should be joyful now; the conquest of Khaybar Castle has just become much easier."

The main battle now began. Both sides attacked with all their force. Ali's sword was struck from his hands, leaving him vulnerable to his enemies. What happened next was nothing short of miraculous. Ali lifted the gigantic castle gate and shouting "*Allahu akbar!* Allah is the greatest!" he ran towards the enemy. Using the castle gate as a shield he quickly repulsed the enemy soldiers who flocked towards him. Witnessing this incredible feat, the Companions shouted for joy. Unable to resist such power, the Jews surrendered, fulfilling the noble Prophet's prediction that Khaybar Castle would be conquered through Ali.

After the battle, a man named Rafi, wondered how it was possible for Ali to lift the enormous castle gate by himself. With seven men, he tried to life the gate but they couldn't even move it off the ground. Later they tried again, adding more and more men each time. At last, they managed to lift the gate; it took forty men to move it.

Pain of

Separation

Ten years had passed since the Messenger of Allah migrated to Medina. In that time, Islam had spread throughout the Arabian peninsula. The last two years had seen thousands of people coming to Medina to accept Islam.

That year, the noble Prophet decided to visit Mecca to perform the Hajj. He invited all the Muslims to join him. Ali was in Yemen fulfilling the mission the Messenger of Allah had given him to invite the people to Islam. As soon as he received the noble Prophet's invitation he set out with a group of new Muslims.

More than one hundred thousand pilgrims gathered in Mecca for the Hajj. This pilgrimage was to be the noble Prophet's last. It was during this pilgrimage that he gave his "Farewell Sermon" where he outlined the main duties of the Muslims.

After the sermon, a new verse was revealed saying, *"Today I have perfected your religion and completed my favor upon you, and I was satisfied that Islam be your religion."*

Following the pilgrimage, the Messenger of Allah returned to Medina where he began to suffer from a severe headache. As time passed, the blessed Prophet's illness increased causing distress to the Muslims. Hearing that his followers were so upset, the Messenger of Allah went to the Masjid al-Nabawi, the mosque in Medina, for the last time, and spoke with his friends. The noble Prophet's Companions did not see him again; from that time onwards he stayed with his family.

The beloved Prophet's illness lasted for thirteen days. At last, the evening time came for the noble Prophet to leave this world and be reunited with Allah.

Abu Bakr, the blessed Prophet's closest friend and most ardent supporter, was drowning in tears. Looking at his beloved Prophet's face for the last time, he said, "O Messenger of Allah, you were beautiful when you were alive and you are even more beautiful in death."

All the Muslims were beside themselves with grief. Umar fainted after shouting, "Whoever says that the Messenger of Allah died, I will cut off his head!"

Abu Bakr addressed the Muslims saying, "O believers, whoever worshipped the Messenger of Allah, know that he passed away. But whoever worshipped Allah should know that he is alive and will never die." Then, he read the verse, "*O Muhammad, verily you will die and they also will die.*"

The death of the noble Prophet caused Ali intense suffering. Due to the Messenger of Allah, Ali had never bowed before an idol. He had learned everything from the blessed Prophet and had experienced everything with him. His death felt like an abandonment and he didn't know what to do. He wandered around in a state of confusion until he heard his name being called, "O Ali, where are you?"

Turning in the direction of the voice, "I'm here," he replied.

"Ali, it's time to fulfil the will of the noble Prophet. It was his will that you prepare him for his last journey."

Without speaking, Ali went to the side of the Messenger of Allah to complete the momentous task of washing his sacred body. Whether it was Ali's tears or the water he poured that washed the body was impossible to tell. According to testament, Ali washed the body and prepared it for burial. While all the Muslims were besides themselves with grief, Ali buried the noble Prophet with a fire raging in his heart.

Fatima, the daughter of the beloved Prophet and wife of Ali, was weeping as if her heart had broken. "How can you pour earth on Allah's Messenger?" she asked Ali. "How can your heart stand it?"

Barely able to suppress his own pain and grief, Ali attempted to comfort his beloved wife.

The noble Prophet was no longer with them. He had returned to Allah the Almighty. The beloved Prophet was the best, kindest and most beautiful of all human beings. He was the honor and pride of humanity. But, as Abu Bakr had reminded everyone, he was a mortal, the same as every human on earth. Now he had gone and the Islamic state was left without a leader.

The Muslims gathered to select a new commander of the faithful. Who would be the new caliph?

Addressing the people, Abu Bakr said, "Dear people, it is in my heart that Umar or Ubayda should be the new caliph."

Umar and Ubayda, may Allah be pleased with them, both rejected the idea at once, "No, dear Abu Bakr; you deserve to be the caliph much more than we do. Give us your hand and let us swear allegiance to you."

All the Muslims in the gathering agreed with this idea and Abu Bakr became the first caliph. The next day, Ali went to Abu Bakr and congratulated him.

Ten-Fold Gain

henever he had the chance, Ali would take his sons, Hasan and Husayn, may Allah be pleased with them, outside and wander around Medina's beautiful areas. On one of these days, the three of them were walking along talking with each other. Hasan and Husayn were asking their father about the places they were visiting and he answered them kindly and patiently. As they were walking, they were approached by an old man who said, "I couldn't find anything to eat today and I'm hungry. Can you help me?"

The man was in a poor condition with ripped clothes. Seeing him, Hasan and Husayn said to their father, "Let's help him. He is hungry."

Ali felt the same as his sons. The man looked like someone who really needed help. As he reached into his pocket, the old man's eyes sparkled with hope and he said to himself, "At last, I have found someone who will help me."

As he felt around his pocket, Ali realized that he had left his money at home. "I forgot to bring money with me," he told the old man.

A hundred different expressions crossed the man's face. He was very upset by this news because he hadn't eaten for a few days. He would never have begged for help if he hadn't been truly desperate.

Seeing his disappointment, Ali said to the old man, "If you can wait, I'll send the children home to get some money."

Feeling ashamed, but having no other hope, the old man said, "I can wait."

Addressing his children, Ali said, "Go home and get the six dirhams I left your mother."

Hasan and Husayn felt very bad about the state of the old man. "Alright, father," they said and ran off towards their house.

When they knocked at the door, their mother, Fatima answered. Seeing them without their father she became worried. "What happened? Where's your father? Is something wrong?" she panicked.

"Our father is waiting for us," they replied. "He wants the six dirhams he gave you this morning."

"What does he want the money for?"

"He will give it to a poor man who is in need," they answered. "Please mother, let's give the money to him."

"Of course, we will give the money to him," she replied. "But, we have no flour at home. Your father gave me the money to buy flour. Go and ask him again. Maybe he forgot that I would buy flour with this money."

The boys ran back to their father who asked, "Did you bring the money?"

Hasan answered, "Father, my mother said you gave her the money for flour and she wants to know if you forgot this?"

Not wanting the man to lose hope, Ali said to his sons, "Go and tell your mother that I will use the money for something more worthwhile."

Running back home again, the children told their mother what their father had said. This time, without saying a word, she handed them the six dirhams.

When they returned with the money, Ali gave it to the poor man who took it and left, giving thanks to Allah.

Ali and his sons walked around for a while longer, then returned home. As they arrived in front of their house, a man leading a camel came over to them. He greeted Ali.

Ali asked the man, "Where are you from and where are you going?"

"I'm going to the bazaar to sell this camel," the man replied. "If you want, I can sell it to you?"

"How much do you want for it?"

"One hundred and forty dirhams," the man answered"

This was a good price for such a nice camel. Ali thought for a while and said, "I would like to buy it but I don't have the money at the moment. If you agree, I will pay you later."

The man answered, "If it was anyone other than you, Ali, I wouldn't accept it. But you are a reliable man. I will sell you this camel and you can pay me later." The man tied the camel to a tree in front of the house and left.

Ali and the children stood looking at the camel. Another man approached and greeted them. He said, "What a nice camel. I need a camel like this. Will you sell it to me?"

"Yes," said Ali.

The man walked over to the camel and started stroking its head. The camel was very happy. "How much do you want for it?" he asked.

"Two hundred dirhams," replied Ali.

"Alright, I'll buy it," the man answered, taking the money out of his wallet and giving it to Ali. He then untied the camel and left.

Ali sent the children inside, then went to pay the man he'd bought the camel from. Walking home again, he was very happy. "Open your hand," he said to Fatima when he arrived home.

Fatima was excited. What could this be? She opened her hands and waited. Ali put the sixty dirhams profit that he had made from selling the camel into her hands. Fatima couldn't believe her eyes,

"Where did all this money come from, Ali? This morning you gave me six dirhams and said it was the last of our money."

"Dear Fatima," Ali replied, "it was the last of our money until I gave it to the poor man."

"What do you mean?"

Ali explained everything that had happened to Fatima, then said, "I once heard from the Messenger of Allah, 'Whoever performs a good deed will receive it back ten-fold.'"

"Do you mean that the good deed you did this morning in giving the poor man that money, has been paid back ten-fold?"

"Exactly!" said Ali.

Ali and Fatima gave thanks to Allah for his generosity.

A Difficult
Task

Caliph Uthman had been martyred by rebels and dark clouds engulfed the holy city of Medina. A new caliph was yet to be chosen and the lack of leadership enabled the rebels to freely roam the city. Uthman's killers were protected by a large group of supporters who also helped to hide the rebels.

Unwilling to take on the huge responsibility of caliph, Ali tried to stay away from the city, spending his days in the date orchards. The people, however, wished to see him as caliph and spoke often about this.

On the fifth day, Ali visited the mosque for the Friday Prayer. Seeing him, the people swore allegiance to him and selected him as their caliph. Present in the mosque were Talha ibn Ubaydullah and Zubayr ibn al-Awwam, may Allah be pleased with them. Previously, they had each been nominated to be caliph, but the people wished for Ali to lead them. They both swore their allegiance to Ali and congratulated him.

Ali became caliph of the Muslims at a very difficult time. There were many issues that needed to be solved. First and most pressing was to find and punish Caliph Uthman's murderers. The people brought up this issue after the Friday Prayer. "O chief of believers," they said, "We know Uthman's killers very well. They killed him and believe it was their right to do so. They must be found and punished."

"I also know what you know," Caliph Ali replied, "but, at this time, the rebels are very powerful. How can I punish them at this time? First, we need to bring peace and then we will find Uthman's killers."

Ali began by changing the governors of the Muslims lands. The Muslim world had descended into strife and new, powerful governors were needed to bring control and order back to these areas. He appointed new leaders in Egypt, Yemen, Basra and

Kufa. The new governor in Damascus, however, was unable to start working as the former governor, Muawiya, objected to Ali's order.

Ali wrote a letter to Muawiya, inviting him to peace but Muawiya returned the letter. He then sent a letter to Ali with his own courier, rejecting his caliphate. Ali was very upset by this letter.

Test

$\mathcal{M}$uawiya's refusal to accept Ali as the caliph resulted in new unrest all around the Islamic state.

At that time, Aisha, may Allah be pleased with her, was in Mecca to perform the Umrah pilgrimage. Hearing about the martyrdom of Caliph Uthman, a huge crowd gathered around her including Talha ibn Ubaydullah and Zubayr ibn al-Awwam. They decided to set out for Basra together. No one could accept the murder of Uthman and, supported by the governors of Mecca and Yemen, they intended to find his killer.

Hearing about this, Ali also set out with his army towards Basra. Neither side intended to fight the other. Approaching Basra, Ali sent his trusted courier, Amir, may Allah be pleased with him, to Aisha. "Why are you here?" he asked.

"I came with the intention of making peace," replied Aisha.

"Dear Aisha," said Amir, "what do you know about peace?"

"I want the killers of Uthman to be found and punished so there will be justice and people will be able to live together in peace," she said.

"O Aisha, the situation is much graver than you realize. With this action you would cause around six hundred people to be killed but then six thousand more would riot and fight. You only want Uthman's killers but six thousand are hiding them. Would you do something that Caliph Ali wouldn't? He also wants to find the killers. He asks you to give him some time. First, let the situation calm down. Come and swear allegiance to him. I fear there will be big trouble because this is a difficult situation."

Aisha listened to Amir and agreed, "If Ali thinks in this way then I agree with him. I hope that this situation will be resolved in a short time before it gets worse."

Amir was happy with his meeting with Aisha and returned to report the good news to Ali. However, there were others among them who were disturbed by this development. Abdullah ibn Saba, the ringleader of the rebels, and his friends, felt that this positive progress should be disrupted and sent men to infiltrate both sides.

Ali, unware of the cunning of Abdullah ibn Saba, entered Basra with his army to spend the night there.

Meanwhile, Aisha and her followers continued to walk close to Hawab where they stopped to rest for the night. During the night, some dogs were heard barking causing Aisha to stir and ask the name of the place they were staying. "This is Hawab, dear Aisha," they replied.

Aisha was shocked. "This is Hawab? Then the dogs are barking for me!" she cried.

"What are you talking about," they asked her, confused.

"Once, my beloved Prophet told me and his wives what will happen to one of us when the dogs in Hawab are barking. O Zubayr, let's pack up and leave this place," she said.

Everyone understood they were in danger, but it was too late. A man approached swiftly on a horse shouting, "Come on! Ali and his army are coming to fight you."

The rider was the ill-intentioned Abdullah ibn Saba, but, due to the darkness of the night, no one recognized him. They packed up and began marching towards Ali's army. It was too late to stop them.

On the other side, another man provoked Ali's army and they too set out for battle. War was inevitable.

At the peak of the violence, Ali approached Zubayr ibn al-Awwam and said, "O Zubayr, do you remember, one day you and I were going to visit the Messenger of Allah and you were smiling at me. The noble Prophet asked you, 'Do you like Ali?' and you answered, 'Yes.' Then, our Prophet said to you, 'But one day, you will be in a situation of harming him and will fight with him.'"

Remembering this, Zubayr became very upset. "Yes, Ali, you remembered that which I forgot," he said, dropping his sword to the ground and turning to leave the battlefield. As he was leaving, he was killed and shortly after Talha ibn Ubaydullah was also felled.

When the battle finally ended, ten thousand people had lost their lives. Ali performed the Funeral Prayer for all the deceased and protected Aisha from any harm. Later, he visited her in Basra where she was staying and when she returned to Medina he ordered the guard regiment to protect her.

Aisha was very sad about the battle. She had played a part in a battle which had seen the deaths of thousands. "I wish I had died before this day," she lamented.

When people asked Ali about the opponent in this unfortunate battle, Ali always replied, "They are all our brothers. For a while, they were against us, but they understood their mistake and apologized, and we forgave them."

Justice

One day, Caliph Ali was wandering through the bazaar, interested in seeing how the traders dealt with one another. Approaching one of them, he asked, "How are you? Do you need anything?"

"No," the trader replied. "I'm very well, thank you."

The bazaar was crowded and noisy. One man was trying to sell some armor, calling out loudly, but no one was showing any interest. Ali walked over to look at the armor and something caught his attention. The armor was very similar to his own. "May I have a look at this armor?" he asked the trader.

"Here you are," said the man. "Take a look."

Ali looked over the armor and the man carried on shouting, "Here! I have armor to sell!"

After examining the armor, Ali was sure that it was his. "This armor belongs to me," he told the man. "You cannot sell it."

The seller recognized Ali but, acting as if he didn't know him, he said "No, this is my armor and I'm trying to sell it."

"This is my armor," Ali insisted. "I lost it a few days ago."

Their discussion began to draw the attention of the people in the bazaar who began to gather round them. Everyone was trying to understand what was happening. Examining the armor closely again, Ali said, "I recognize it from the sword scratches. This is my armor."

"The sword scratches could be on any armor," argued the trader. "You cannot prove that this armor is yours."

"Then let's go to the court," said Ali. "The judge can decide between us."

The trader was reluctant but, seeing the angry faces around him, he accepted, "Alright, let's go."

Ali and the trader stood before the judge. Addressing the judge, the trader began, "I'm a Christian. I'm not a Muslim. Therefore, I'm afraid you will not judge fairly."

"It doesn't matter which religion you are from," replied the judge. "I decide in favor of who is in the right."

Despite this assurance, the trader was still concerned because his opponent was the powerful caliph.

Ali was the first to start his defense, "This armor belongs to me. I lost it a few days ago."

"Do you have two witnesses to testify for you?" the judge asked.

"Yes, I do. If you wish, I can go and get them."

The judge gave Ali permission to leave the court. Shortly after, he returned with his son, Hasan, and his servant.

The judge objected, "Well, Ali, your servant can be a witness but not your son. You must bring another witness."

"How can this be?" said Ali. "Everyone knows how reliable Hasan is."

"Yes, I also know this very well, Ali. But, according to Islamic law, a father and son cannot be witnesses for each other."

Observing the proceedings, the trader was shocked. He had imagined that the judge would not be fair in the case of the caliph against a mere tradesman. He never imagined he would witness the judge interrogating the caliph and not allowing his witness. He called out to the judge, "Please, stop!"

All eyes turned to the tradesman. Continuing, he said, "This armor does belong to Caliph Ali. One day I was behind him while he was riding his camel. His armor fell down but he did not realize. I took the armor before anyone noticed, but I really regret my actions."

Everyone in the courtroom was relieved that the matter was finally resolved, but the trader had not finished. Obtaining permission to speak some more, he continued, "I understand that the Islamic religion is good and that Muslims are fair. A powerful caliph was unable to take what rightfully belonged to him from a Christian trader. The judge did not accept the witness of the caliph who is the head of the Islamic State. I want to become a Muslim."

The man made his declaration of faith and became Muslim. Ali was very pleased at this turn of events. Congratulating the man, he presented him with the armor as a gift and also promised him a horse.

Time for Farewell

Caliph Ali was greatly saddened and worn out by the battle in Basra and the incident of the armor as well as many other troubles. Only a person raised by the noble Prophet himself could endure such difficulties and still endeavor to fulfil his duties perfectly. But, Ali was unaware that a dangerous plan was being hatched against him.

Abdullah ibn Muljam and two accomplices were planning to kill Ali. They didn't worry what would happen to them afterwards; their intention was to avenge their brothers who had died in the battle of Basra. "Even if we die while trying to get justice," they thought, "when we kill the leader of the State, we will get revenge for our brothers."

After planning for days, the two accomplices set out to kill the governor, Muawiya, and the state assistant, Amr ibn As. Abdullah ibn Muljam made his way to Kufa to kill Ali.

It was early on a Friday morning. Ali, calling his family to rise for the Morning Prayer, set out in the dark towards the mosque. He heard footsteps approaching from behind, and naturally assumed it was someone heading to the mosque to pray. This person, however, was Abdullah ibn Muljam. Catching up with Ali, he struck him several times with his poisoned sword.

The people nearby realized what had happened and, while some rushed to help Ali, others caught the killer. "Leave me here and go and pray," Ali implored. "Don't miss the Prayer and tell the people inside not to leave their Prayers either."

With blood flowing from his wounds, Ali pointed at Abdullah ibn Muljam and through his pain said, "Keep in him prison and treat him well. If I survive, I will think about what to do with him. But, if I die, take his life for mine."

Ali was taken to his house. After a while, unable to hold onto life, he recited the verse, "*Whoever makes goodness, he will find goodness. Whoever makes evil, he will find evil.*" At the age of sixty-three, he closed his eyes for the last time.

Before he died, Ali said to his son, Hasan, "My dear son! Listen to my advice. The greatest wealth is intelligence and the greatest poverty is foolishness. The greatest loneliness is arrogance and the greatest magnanimity is good morality. Beware of befriending a foolish man because he will harm you while trying to help you. Beware of friendships with stingy people because they will take you away from what you need. Success is the best guide and good morality is your best friend."